ASPECTS OF GEOGRAPHY

General Editors: J. H. Johnson and Ian Douglas

Desert Geomorphology

ANDREW GOUDIE AND ANDREW WATSON

School of Geography, Oxford University

SECOND EDITION

M
MACMILLAN

First edition 1980
Second edition 1990

Published by
MACMILLAN EDUCATION LTD
Houndmills, Basingstoke, Hampshire RG21 2XS
and London
Companies and representatives throughout the world

Printed in Hong Kong

British Library Cataloguing in Publication Data
Goudie, Andrew
Desert geomorphology. – 2nd ed.
1. Deserts. Geomorphology
I. Title   II. Watson, Andrew, 1954–   III. Series
551.4
ISBN 0–333–52065–3

Acknowledgements

The authors and publishers wish to thank the following who have kindly given permission for the use of copyright material:

Batsford for a figure from R. U. Cooke & A. Warren, *Geomorphology of Deserts*, and Cambridge University Press for a figure from A. S. Goudie & J. C. Wilkinson, *The Warm Desert Environment*.

The publishers have made every effort to trace copyright holders, but if they have inadvertently overlooked any they will be pleased to make the necessary arrangements at the first opportunity.

Cover photo by kind permission J. Allan Cash.

Contents

Preface

In recent years, geography has been changing with great speed. It is not primarily that the basic facts of geographical distributions are themselves changing, although, of course, this has happened. It is far more that geographers have come to think differently about the significance of geographical distributions, about how to study them, and about what topics are worthy objects of geographical investigation.

Nobody can remain in close touch with the expanding frontier of geographical knowledge at all its points. New developments in geography are the subject of contributions to learned journals, but these are difficult to track down and, even when found, they are difficult for the non-specialist to assess. Nor can all new developments be taken up quickly by the standard textbooks, which must necessarily go some years between revisions. As a result, *Aspects of Geography* has been organised as a series of concise reports by writers who are in contact with a particular sector of the subject's development. Although the series is particularly aimed at A level students and their teachers it is hoped that the series will also be useful to college and university students as an introduction to the various specialist fields that will be covered.

The existence of specialist texts would make any attempt in this volume to cover all desert landforms and all desert processes an impossible venture. The authors have assumed that readers know something of the distribution, the locations and the environmental conditions of the world's deserts, and the intention in this volume is to concentrate on recent developments and popular misconceptions.

The emphasis which is adopted here, and the explanations proposed, offer a consistent and defensible approach to desert landscapes. The suggested balance between forms inherited from past environments and features in balance with contemporary processes is one which seems to offer the soundest explanation of the rather complicated landforms of the world's deserts.

This second edition has been extensively revised. The authors have expanded and updated the work and have added chapters illustrating the nature of the human impact on deserts and discussing the application of research in desert geomorphology.

J. H. JOHNSON
IAN DOUGLAS

1. The great variety of desert landscapes

The deserts of the world, which occur in every continent including Antarctica, are areas where there is a great deficit of moisture, predominantly because rainfall levels are low. In some deserts this situation is in part also the result of high temperatures, which mean that evaporation rates are high. Whereas even the driest parts of Britain have around 500 mm of rainfall per year, there are many desert weather stations that normally record less than one tenth of that figure, and in some years they may even fail to receive any rain at all. It is this shortage of moisture which determines many of the characteristics of the soils, the vegetation, the landforms, the animals, and the activities of humans.

Not all desert areas, however, are as deficient in moisture as some of the others: aridity is a matter of degree, and the degree of aridity in different types of desert is basic to an understanding of desert geomorphology. One of the most used subdivisions was made by a scientist called Meigs who divided arid lands into three types: the extremely arid (covering about 4 per cent of the Earth's surface); the arid (covering about 15 per cent) and the semi-arid (also covering about 15 per cent). Combined, these amount to 34 per cent of the Earth's land surface area. The extremely arid areas are defined as being those with a record of at least twelve consecutive months without rainfall and where there is no regular seasonal rhythm of precipitation, while the other two sub-divisions are based on the extent of the difference between precipitation and potential evapo-transpiration (the moisture deficit). Certainly, no single rainfall value can be used to delimit the desert lands, because of the role of temperature and other factors. In Australia, for instance, areas in the hot, tropical north-west of the country receiving some 500 mm of annual rainfall are within the arid zone, whereas in the cooler southern parts of the country the boundary of the desert may be approximated by the 250 mm isohyet.

Thus one can recognise a wide range of desert types according to their degree of aridity. It is also useful to remember that there is a difference between warm deserts and those deserts which because of high latitude or high altitude have winter frosts. Likewise, coastal deserts, such as the Namib of south western Africa (Namibia) or the

Atacama of western South America, will have rather uniform temperatures and much higher humidity characteristics from the deserts of continental interiors.

Since, on the basis of climatic characteristics one third of the Earth's land surface can be classified as desert, it is to be expected that there should be a great diversity of desert landscapes. Just as the temperate regions of the world comprise such features as mountains and plains, lakes, rivers and deltas, so deserts have corresponding topographic features. Any classification of the major deserts of the world may first be divided into those relief units determined by geological factors and then subdivided into those which are distinctive owing to more specifically geomorphic factors. So, for example, while one can distinguish between shield deserts and mountain-and-basin deserts, on a more detailed scale these may be subdivided into sand deserts, stony deserts, clay plains and riverine deserts.

Mountain ranges and their associated basins make up between 40 and 50 per cent of the land surface of the Saharan, Arabian and south-western United States deserts. Though the overall relief is a product of tectonics, the landscape is modified by the desert climate, which is itself a little unusual since mountainous areas in deserts frequently receive more rainfall than the surrounding low-lying areas and may be cool enough to experience occasional frost. These mountains may act as the source areas for rivers, while large ranges such as the Hoggar and Tibesti in the Sahara were well vegetated at times during the Pleistocene.

The mountain-and-basin deserts are often undergoing present-day mountain building, and these tectonic processes create sharp fault junctions between mountains and plains. One of the finest examples of this type of desert is the fault-block topography of the arid lands of the south-western United States. In Death Valley, one of the hottest and driest places on Earth, high mountains rising to over 3000 m are close neighbours of salt flats which lie below sea level. The high relative relief is one of the major controls of the types of geomorphological processes that operate.

The shield deserts which occur in India, Africa, Arabia and Australia have much less relief than the mountain-and-basin deserts, and this is rarely enough to lead to a moderation of aridity or to introduce forms which result from current frost action. They are also areas where tectonic activity has been less so that ancient landforms have often survived. In addition, they appear in some cases to have been influenced only slightly by climatic changes in the Pleistocene. Indeed, the Namib Desert appears to have been in existence ever since an Antarctic ice sheet cooled the waters of the Benguela current in the Miocene.

Within desert regions of these two major structural types there are some areas which are dominated by erosion, some which are dominated by deposition, some which are dominated by water action, some which are dominated by wind action, some which are zones of salt accumulation and some which are zones of salt removal. The nature and location of the processes which operate are strongly influenced by topographic situation. Thus Mabbutt has described various major physiographic settings:

desert uplands where geological controls of relief are important, bedrock is exposed, and relief is high;

desert piedmonts which are transitional zones separated from the uplands by a break of gradient but nonetheless receiving runoff and sediments from the uplands. Both erosional and depositional forms may prevail here, including alluvial fans (see p. 12) and pediments (see p. 43);

stony deserts which comprise stony plains and structural plateaux formed at lower levels and which may have a cover of stone pavement (see p. 41);

desert rivers and floodplains, which are a further feature of desert lowlands;

desert lake basins (usually salty) which are the sumps to which the disorganised drainage progresses; and

sand deserts which tend to be beyond the limits of active fluvial processes but which often derive their materials by wind action on floodplains or lake basins.

Finally, it is worth remembering that as the desert margins are approached and rainfall amounts increase so the nature of the landforms changes. In particular, the development of a more continuous vegetation cover leads to a great change in the operation of geomorphic processes, in the balance between wind and water, and in the balance between chemical and physical processes of weathering. It is, therefore, worth making a distinction between areas of extreme aridity and areas of semi-aridity.

In truly arid deserts, there is very little vegetation cover; in semi-arid areas roots are fairly continuous (to acquire sufficient moisture) but surface vegetation is scattered and discontinuous; beyond the desert margin the surface vegetation cover is more or less continuous as one moves into the steppe grasslands or savanna.

The processes of weathering, erosion and sedimentation may be basically the same in all deserts, but landscapes as diverse as the Basin-and-Range Province of the south-western United states, the plains-and-inselberg of the Central Namib, the chott-and-erg of Algeria and Tunisia, and the hammada-and-erg of the Hoggar are produced. The variety results, on the largest scale, from geological factors such as tectonics and rock type and also climate, particularly rainfall and wind regimes. The diversity is maintained by the physical process active in the deserts and the extent to which the effectiveness of contemporary erosional processes has replaced forms surviving from the different environments of the past.

2. Water action in desert landscapes

Precipitation and runoff

On pages 23 to 37 we make it clear that wind action is important in moulding desert relief, while on pages 38 to 40 we indicate that climatic change means that water action has been potent in the past periods of pluvial conditions. In this chapter we show that in many desert areas contemporary water action is of great significance in shaping desert features in spite of the apparent shortage of moisture.

While desert rainfall totals are low, desert rainfall is highly variable over time so that totals in some years may be quite high. This inter-annual variability (V) can be expressed as a simple index:

$$V\% = \frac{\text{the mean deviation from the average}}{\text{the average}} \times 100$$

European humid temperate stations such as Rome have a precipitation variability of less than 20 per cent whereas variability in the Sahara ranges from 80 to 150 per cent.

Statistical analysis of discharge records also demonstrates the extreme variability of river flows in arid lands. Values for selected arid and non-arid areas are shown in Table 1.

Area	V% of annual flows
(a) *Arid areas*	
Australia	127
East Mediterranean	125
North America	65
South Africa	114
(b) *Non-arid areas*	
Australia	67
North America	30
Europe	20
Asia	20

Table 1 Hydrological variability of surface runoff in selected areas

In addition to showing year to year variability, the rainfall of desert regions is known to undergo longer term fluctuations that may last for a few decades or so.

Figure 1 shows annual rainfall curves for certain arid zone stations between 1945 and 1974. Certain stations (e.g. Jodhpur and Phoenix) show high variability from year to year but no consistent trend, whereas other stations (e.g. Alice Springs, Abéché and Agadez) seem to have experienced an apparent downward trend in rainfall. Changes have been especially dramatic in the Sahara and neighbouring sub-Saharan zones (Figure 2a). Wet conditions were widespread in the 1950s, with decadal averages ranging from 15 per cent above normal in the southern areas to 35 to 40 per cent above normal along the Saharan fringe. Such favourable conditions came to an end in the 1960s and by 1968 the drought was beginning in earnest. Deficits for the six years 1968 to 1973 averaged 15 to 40 per cent below the mean. There was a slight amelioration in the mid-1970s, which tempted some observers to suggest that the drought had ended, but large rainfall deficits returned between 1976 and 1987. Although the latest Sahel drought has been especially serious, other lengthy dry spells have occurred twice before in this century, around 1912 and in the early 1940s.

Such variability in precipitation is reflected in changes in river discharges and lake areas. Figure 2b shows how the discharge data for the Senegal River in West Africa broadly parallel the rainfall fluctuations we have just discussed, with three periods of specially low flow in this century. The low flows since 1968 have had serious consequences for irrigation schemes. Likewise, Lake Chad has shown a systematic decrease of its level. Between 1963 and 1973 its surface area had diminished by over 65 per cent and its volume decreased by 75 per cent.

Over shorter time-scales there are records of individual storms of surprising size in desert areas, storms that have generated considerable runoff. For example, at Chicama in Peru in 1925, where the mean annual precipitation over previous years was a paltry 4 mm, 394 mm fell in one storm. Similarly, at El Djem in Tunisia (mean annual precipitation, 275 mm), 319 mm fell in three days in September 1969. Such events are capable of producing great geomorphic activity when they occur, but they are too rare to be the main influence shaping the landforms.

However, we must not suggest that all desert rainfall occurs as storms of great intensity. This is brought out clearly when one

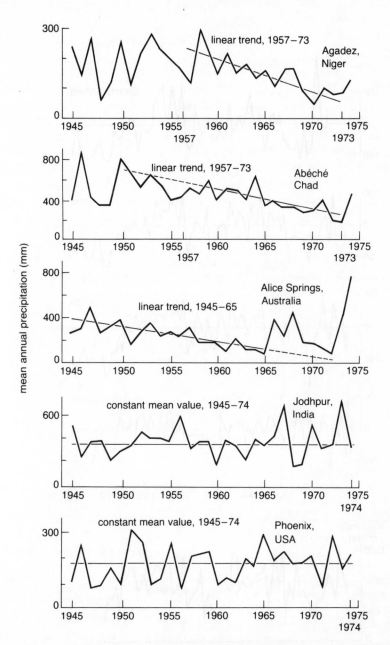

Figure 1 Rainfall variations at selected arid zone stations between 1945 and 1974

(a)

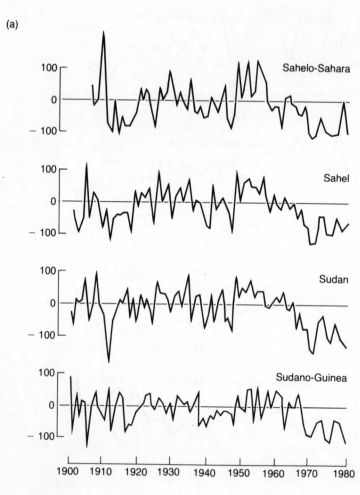

(b)

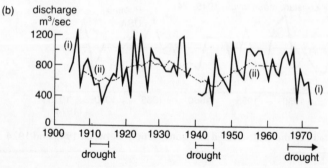

considers the rainfall statistics for Death Valley in California, and for the Jordan Desert (Figure 3). Both these areas have very low rainfall in terms of mean annual levels (67.1 mm and 80.8 mm respectively), yet on average rain falls in 17 days and 26 days respectively in the year, so that the mean rainfall in each rainfall event in Death Valley is 3.9 mm. London's average rainy day has 4 mm.

Thus most desert rainfall occurs in storms of low intensity, yet occasional 'flash floods' cause disruption to communications and even loss of life. If the relatively frequent generation of such floods cannot be attributed to anything exceptional about desert rainfall, then the answer must lie in the balance between infiltration and runoff. Many desert soils have characteristics which enable them to generate considerable runoff from quite low rainfall intensities (Figure 4). First, the sparse vegetation cover provides little organic litter on the surface to absorb water. Second, the lack of vegetation means that humus levels in the soil are low and this, combined with the minimal disturbance by plant roots and a greatly reduced soil animal population, makes the soils dense and compact in texture. Third, the virtual absence of interception by a plant cover allows rain to beat down on the surface with maximum force, and fine soil particles, unbound by vegetation, are re-distributed by splash to lodge in pore-spaces and to create a puddled soil surface of reduced permeability. In some cases, the presence of certain clay minerals which expand in volume upon being wetted (such as montmorillo-nite) will further clog the fissures and pore spaces in the soil zone. Studies in the Negev in Israel have shown that where such crusted and impermeable soils exist the infiltration rate is no more than 2 mm/hour, so that a rate in excess of this is likely to produce overland flow.

It is also a paradox that in some desert areas the greatest quantities of run-off appear to be generated by storms falling on low angle slopes, in contrast to conditions on vegetated hillslopes in humid regions. The explanation for this seems to be that steep desert slopes tend to be mantled with coarse debris which is a greater impediment

Figure 2 Rainfall and river discharge fluctuations in West Africa in the twentieth century. (a) Annual rainfall as a % of the mean for four sub-Saharan zones (after the work of Sharon Nicholson). (b) The discharge of the Senegal River at Bakel (15° N, 12° W) (i) is the record of mean annual discharge, and (ii) is the ten year moving mean of discharge

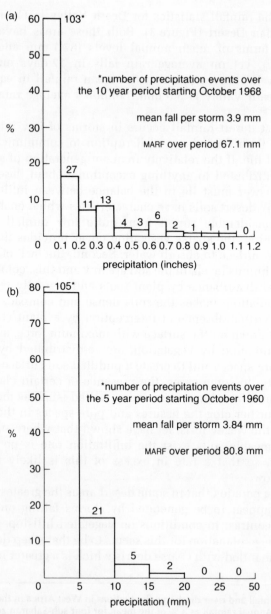

Figure 3 Histograms showing the percentage frequency of rainfall amounts per rainy day in (a) Death Valley, California, USA, (b) H4 in the Jordanian Desert, Middle East (MARF = mean annual rainfall)

to runoff and does not become compacted in the way described above. Low angle slopes tend to be covered by soils subject to compaction (and thus low permeability), while the finer material in turn provides a smoother surface which facilitates runoff.

Sediment yield and concentration

One useful measure of geomorphological activity is sediment yield per unit area over a period of time. For rivers this can be determined either by the measurement of suspended sediment from drainage basins or by recording the quantity of sediment accumulation in reservoirs. Studies suggest that in deserts, as precipitation rises from zero, sediment yield increases at a rapid rate because more runoff becomes available to move sediment and yet there is still bare ground susceptible to rainwash erosion. As the amount of vegetation cover increases, sediment yields start to decline. Thus, while in

Figure 4 Silty desert surfaces have low infiltration capacities, so that when a shower occurs, as in the catchment of this small *wadi* in Bahrain, runoff occurs rapidly, and may transport large volumes of sediment

extreme deserts sediment yields are very small, in semi-arid areas they may be among the highest in the world (Figure 5).

The high concentrations of sediment in runoff from desert uplands reflect the vulnerability of unvegetated surfaces to water erosion. Desert streams, when they flow, tend to be turbid and there are frequent occurrences of mud flows in which solid matter may account for between 25 and 75 per cent of the flow and the viscosity is so high that large boulders can be carried. Such large sediment concentrations are important in the formation of alluvial fans, and can lead to rapid sedimentation behind engineering structures such as dams.

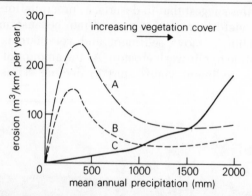

Figure 5 Sediment yield in relation to mean annual precipitation. A represents rates of erosion in high relief situations, B represents rates of erosion in lower relief situations, C represents rates of limestone solution. Rates of erosion appear to be at a maximum under semi-arid conditions, whereas rates of solution only become high under conditions of much more substantial rainfall

Alluvial fans

One of the main features produced by water action in deserts is the alluvial fan – a cone of sediment that occurs between a mountain front and a low-lying plain. They vary greatly in size from 10 m in radius to more than 20 km, and many large fans are thicker than 300 m at the apex. Most fans form in situations where a river emerges from its confined mountain course (or canyon). At such a point the river can spread out, dissipating energy and decreasing its velocity, so that deposition of sediment occurs. They are not normally the result of a sharp reduction in slope between a

Figure 6 Some arid areas have very high drainage densities as a result of the presence of erodible materials with low infiltration capacities, a very limited vegetation cover, and occasional storms. (a) This heavily dissected landscape is the famous Badlands of South Dakota, USA. (b) Characteristic 'organ-pipe' erosional features in a gully developed in colluvial fan sediments in Swaziland, Southern Africa

supposedly steep mountain section and a flat plain section, but their presence is facilitated in areas of tectonic disturbance where there has been a base-level fall in the area of deposition relative to the source area. Alluvial fans along a mountain front can join laterally; in North America this is commonly called a *bajada*.

Fans tend to be rather unstable environments, for the aggrading streams that make them are prone to change their positions on the fan surface, and there may also be phases of relatively rapid incision and phases of relatively rapid aggradation. This can pose hazards for human occupance.

Drainage networks

Because of high runoff and sediment yield from some desert slopes, the imprint of water is often made clear through the development of a considerable degree of *dissection* or high *drainage density* (the total length of stream channels per unit area) (Figure 6). On soft rocks *badlands* may develop and these often have drainage densities between ten and twenty times the average range under humid climates. In much of Britain, on sedimentary rocks the drainage density is 2–8 km/km^2 while in parts of arid North America it can be as high as 350 km/km^2. However, in sandy areas in deserts, where surface conditions give a high infiltration rate and hence little runoff, drainage density will be very low.

3. Weathering

Desert weathering tends to be both superficial and highly selective in how it attacks different rocks, but while the presence of split boulders, exfoliation sheets and other forms attest to the operation of weathering processes, it is all too easy to miss the main process involved if the only evidence is the appearance of the weathered rock.

Traditionally, much of the weathering in deserts has been attributed to mechanical or physical processes. In particular, great stress used to be placed on the role of the alternation of the daytime heat and nocturnal cold (*insolation weathering*), and it was believed that the process would be favoured by the different coefficients of expansion of different minerals. It was believed that daily heating and cooling under the extreme conditions present in deserts could lead to rock fracture, and there have been many reports in the literature of rocks splitting with a noise like a pistol shot. A desert traveller, Uwe George, wrote: 'Especially during the hot summer months, a traveller in the mountains of the desert is likely to hear a constant series of reports caused by bursting stones. Gaping cracks as much as 30 feet long can form in the rock. I remember once resting near a large rock about 3 feet wide when it suddenly gave a loud report, like a cannon being fired and shattered into several pieces.' (*In the Deserts of this Earth*, Hamish Hamilton, 1978).

Attempts to simulate this process in the laboratory have in general failed to create rock fracture and this has cast doubt on whether insolation weathering really operates effectively. Nonetheless many of the experiments have been criticised recently on various grounds: the heating tests were necessarily carried out on unconfined rock samples, free to expand and contract as a whole; the samples used have by necessity been small cubes and samples of larger dimensions would suffer markedly larger thermal stress; the cycles of heating and cooling employed were highly artificial and, moreover, the phenomenon of rock fatigue may have been overlooked. The case against insolation weathering, therefore, is not conclusive.

The case for another form of physical weathering in desert environments – *salt weathering* – is easier to establish. Rock surfaces in deserts are commonly impregnated with soluble salts because evaporation exceeds rainfall, and such salts can disintegrate rocks by two main processes: the growth of crystals from solutions, and the expansion of hygroscopic salts on hydration. Many laboratory experiments have demonstrated the power of these processes and they have been shown to lead to the breaking of building stones and other materials. The widespread splitting that occurs where sediments are delivered into a saline environment is nowhere better exemplified than in Death Valley, California (see Figure 7).

The upper photograph shows the nature of the cobbles that make up the alluvial fan sediments in Death Valley before the salt zone is reached. They are large, solid and well rounded. The middle photograph, taken just where the salt zone meets the fan, shows that disintegration is well advanced, while the bottom photograph, taken well into the salt zone, shows that disintegration is virtually complete. This transformation has been achieved over a horizontal distance of only a few hundred metres.

In some desert environments, other physical processes causing rock disintegration may be effective. For example, in cold deserts or in mountains with some winter rainfall, frost action may cause rock splitting, while in other cases rock fracture may result through the release of confining pressures with the removal of overlying rock. This latter cause is not in any sense restricted to deserts.

The effectiveness of chemical weathering in deserts is severely reduced by the lack of water in the desert environment. Nonetheless, it should be remembered that in deserts moisture is not totally absent: dew can occur with great frequency; in coastal deserts moist fogs may occur on more than 100 days in the year, while, as we have seen, even in deserts with only a small annual rainfall of 70 to 80 mm, rain falls on about 20 days in the year. Moreover, when moisture is known to be present, weathering appears to proceed at a relatively fast rate. Thus shaded sites, and sites within reach of soil moisture, seem to undergo greater weathering, and experimental work in the laboratory has shown that 'insolation' weathering rates are greatly accelerated when rock cooling is achieved by a fine water spray rather than by dry air cooling. As one moves into higher rainfall zones on the margin of deserts the presence of greater moisture and greater organic activity means that chemical weathering becomes more important, with the result that soils tend to contain more clay, to be less saline and to have better horizon development.

One consequence of chemical weathering of desert rock outcrops is that they are frequently stained dark by a substance called *desert varnish* (Figure 8). This is largely composed of oxides of iron and

Figure 7 In Death Valley pebbles break down very rapidly once they come into the highly saline environment of the playa bottom

manganese that have been precipitated on or in the top few microns of the rock surface, possibly as a result of bacterial action. Recent work on the dating of desert varnish may provide a valuable tool for establishing the chronology of climatic fluctuations in many arid and semi-arid regions.

Figure 8 In many desert areas rock surfaces are coated with a thin patina called desert varnish. Where this has been scratched away, as with these graffiti in Karakoram Mountains in northern Pakistan, the lighter underlying rock is evident

4. Desert crusts

Deserts are frequently characterised as regions which are divided into two distinct types of environment: erosional and depositional. One finds intense weathering of bedrock by such agents as salt and heat followed by erosion of the debris by wind and water. The other environment experiences large-scale deposition in the form of such phenomena as sand seas or alluvial fan deposits. There is, however, a third type of environment where these processes of erosion and sedimentation appear greatly retarded or even inactive. This zone is characterised by desert crusts which themselves have a wide variety of forms; true desert crusts are materials cemented by 'soluble' materials.

Once consolidation and cementation have taken place the crust protects the underlying sediments from erosion. In this way former *pediments* (see p. 43), as in the area peripheral to the salt lakes of southern Tunisia, have been preserved. In some instances, the presence of a crust can result in the formation of *buttes* or *mesas* since it acts as a protective cap rock. Local inversion of relief may occur when a crust which has developed in a low-lying pan protects the sediments from deflation relative to the surrounding unconsolidated materials to produce an upstanding block.

There are a number of different types of hard crust (duricrust) associated with warm desert environments. The main types are subdivided by their cement to give calcrete (also known as caliche), silcrete, gypsum crusts (gypcrete) and sodium chloride crusts. All these types may be subdivided into different forms according to structure, chemistry and origin.

Calcretes, calcium carbonate crusts, are the most widely distributed desert crusts and are found in almost all the warm arid and semi-arid zones. The numerous different forms that have been described include indurated horizons up to 40 m thick composed of cemented boulders, gravels, sands or silts, and also accumulations of calcareous nodules and powdery calcretes. Transitions from hardpan near the surface through a nodular zone to a powdery horizon are common.

Silcretes are crusts formed by cementation of a matrix by silica in the form of opal, chalcedony, quartz or mixtures of these depending on the stage of development. As in the case of calcrete, the indurated component of a silcrete profile is the most significant feature in terms of the effect on landscape evolution. This hardpan, however, is frequently only a small component of a complete silcrete profile, some of which may be up to 100 m thick. The most extensive areas of silcrete are found in southern Africa and Australia. Silcretes are by no means restricted to semi-arid areas and, unlike the other desert crusts described here, possibly also form in relatively wet sub-tropical areas.

Gypsum (calcium sulphate) and sodium chloride crusts have received far less attention from geomorphologists than either calcretes or silcretes. Pedologists have studied gypsum and sodium chloride-rich soils in the USA, USSR and North Africa since they pose severe difficulties to agricultural development. However, the geomorphic significance of crusts up to 10 m thick covering large areas of the Sahara, Namib and Australian deserts, has not been studied.

There have been a number of attempts to establish the environmental controls responsible for these different desert crusts. Most of these attempts have concentrated on the significance of rainfall on the distributional characteristics. Calcretes predominate in areas where rainfall is 200 to 500 mm, while gypsum crusts are found in zones with less than about 200 mm but usually more than 50 mm. Sodium chloride crusts, other than those formed by evaporation or surface waters, are found in areas with less than 50 mm of rainfall. The reason for this distribution would appear to be related to the solubility of the various minerals involved, each mineral having a threshold above which the climate is wet enough to dissolve and leach the near-surface accumulations.

The processes involved in the origin of these desert crusts are as diverse as the crusts themselves. They may be divided into five broad groups, each of which may account for certain forms of the crusts.

1 The *lacustrine* model, which involves precipitation of minerals from an evaporating water body, is appropriate to certain gypsum and sodium chloride crusts found in closed basins, and also some calcareous deposits. Yet the characteristic layered structure of these deposits is not in evidence in most crusts. Indeed, the topographic location of many crusts precludes a lacustrine origin.

2 Models of *in situ* development of crusts involve a *relative* accumulation of the cementing or dominant mineral by the leaching of other minerals. The processes are particularly relevant to certain silcretes and calcretes which have apparently developed in weathering profiles. The processes involved vary according to the original material undergoing decomposition and the type of crust produced. The removal of other components of the bedrock or regolith matrix through chemical alteration and/or leaching results in the relative increase in silica or calcium carbonate.

3 A broad category of models, involving the accumulation of minerals by upward movement of these in ground-water or soil moisture, has many proponents. Some calcretes and gypsum crusts are produced by precipitation of the minerals at the surface of a fluctuating ground-water table. There are, however, many examples of crusts which have developed on slopes of 20° or more and on hill crests. These cannot have been precipitated from the water table since water tables do not parallel the land surface so precisely. Furthermore, soil scientists have shown that capillary rise of water through soil is limited to a few centimetres. Hence, in many desert areas where the water table is very deep, the surface crusts cannot have originated in this way unless they are very old features.

4 *Lateral movement of minerals* has been suggested as a possible mechanism for the development of Australian silcretes. The model may explain crusts developed in valleys or large basins where waters accumulate and, as they evaporate, precipitate the minerals which were brought into solution as the waters seeped through the soil and bedrock of the upper drainage basin. Calcium carbonate cemented pediment fans form thick calcretes in many areas (sometimes termed fanglomerates). Lateral movement of gypsum dust by deflation from large salt lakes has been proposed to account for the material making up the gypsum crusts of southern Tunisia. This model can account for the topographic location of these crusts on steep slopes and hill crests but requires modification in cases where the crusts have evidently formed beneath the surface.

5 Sub-surface accumulations, excluding the weathering crusts (*in situ*) and those formed at the top of a water table, can be placed in a category of *pedogenic crusts*. Though some processes of pedogenic accumulation of minerals involve capillary rise of water, most involve a net downward movement by leaching. Rain water will leach minerals present at the surface and in the upper soil horizons to a greater depth. The soluble minerals may be there within wind-blown sand or loess, in salts deposited by fog moisture, or may even be present in the rain water. In an arid environment, the water from any one storm will simply replace the soil moisture deficit created during the preceding dry period. Hence, in an area where potential evaporation exceeds rainfall, it is unlikely that any water will move out of the base of the soil zone unless the rainfall is markedly seasonal or the soil has a low moisture storage capacity.

After rainfall, evaporation of the soil moisture proceeds from the surface downward, precipitating the dissolved minerals. Over numerous such cycles the surface horizons will be leached and the lower soil zone cemented by the precipitated minerals. These sub-surface crusts may be exposed when the overlying leached horizon is stripped by deflation or other forms of erosion.

5. Sand dunes

Under conditions of low rainfall, as are found in deserts, vegetation cover is limited so that unconsolidated surface materials are more easily moved by the wind. Grains of sand may be winnowed from alluvial deposits, from lakeshores, from seashores, and from weathered rocks like sandstone and granite, and are then carried across the desert surface. Locally this sand, which becomes well sorted during transport, is deposited as great ergs or fields of regularly formed sand dunes (Figure 9). About one-third to one-quarter of the world's deserts are covered by wind-blown sand though in some deserts, notably the North American, dunes may in fact cover only a small portion (1 to 2 per cent) of the area.

When wind velocity exceeds the threshold velocity required to initiate sand movement (generally this is about 20 km per hour) sand grains begin to roll along the ground, but after a short distance this

Figure 9 Sand dunes in the Wahiba Sands of Oman. Note the development of ripples in the foreground, the sparse nature of the vegetation, and the broad deflated plain between two parallel dunes

gives rise to a bounding or jumping action called *saltation*. G
are taken up a small distance into the airstream (often only a m
of a few centimetres) and then fall back to the ground in a fairl
trajectory. The descending grains dislodge further particle:
thereby the process of saltation is maintained. The saltating g
(which generally have a diameter between about 0.15 and 0.25
and form about 70 to 75 per cent of the total mass of moving sana,
hit larger grains (with diameters generally in the range of 0.25 to
2.0 mm) which may then be moved forward by a process termed
surface creep which accounts for about 20 to 25 per cent of the sand
in motion. It should be noted, however, that the saltating and
creeping grain populations are not necessarily independent. The
smallest grains of sand (between 0.05 and 0.15 mm in diameter) may
be carried high up into the air in *suspension*, and this accounts for
about 5 per cent of the material moved by the wind. The growth of
dunes, as Mabbutt (1977, p. 223) has explained, 'follows from the
tendency for saltating sand to accumulate in areas already sand-
covered in preference to adjoining sand-free surfaces. This results
from the check to a strong wind through intensified sand movement
over a sand surface and from the lower rate of sand movement where
saltating grains splash into loose sand compared with that over firm
ground'.

The geometric forms of deposition of sand as dunes are very varied
(Figure 10) and depend on the supply of sand, the nature of the wind
regime, the extent of vegetation cover, and the shape of the ground
surface. Thus, for example, the great longitudinal parallel dune
systems require sufficient sand to allow the growth of continuous

Figure 10 E. D. McKee and his collaborators have used satellite imagery to map
the different types of dune found in the world's major deserts. The major classes
that they encountered are shown here, together with their formative wind
directions (shown by the arrows). Barchans are crescentic-shaped individual dunes.
The horns of the crescent point downwind. Barchanoid ridges are asymmetric
waves, oriented transverse to the wind direction, which consist of coalesced
barchans in rows. They have a steeply dipping lee slope. Transverse dunes also form
normal to the dominant wind direction but lack barchanoid structures. Dome
dunes form where dune height is inhibited by unobstructed strong winds. They lack
a steep slip face. Linear dunes are parallel, straight dunes with slip faces on both
sides and with their length many times greater than their width. Blowouts result
from erosion of a pre-existing sand sheet, while parabolics represent a type of
blowout in which the middle part has moved forward with respect to the sides or
arms. In areas of complex winds, dunes may have a starlike form while, in areas
with winds from two opposing directions, reversing dunes may form. In addition to
these simple forms, more complex patterns combine various elements (Goudie 1985)

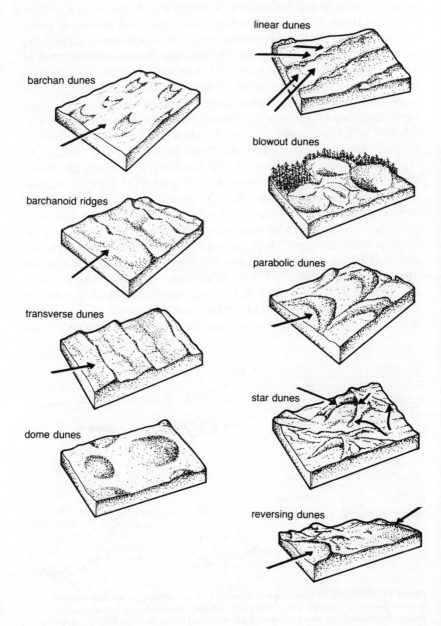

barchan dunes

barchanoid ridges

transverse dunes

dome dunes

linear dunes

blowout dunes

parabolic dunes

star dunes

reversing dunes

...lerably regular surface to permit the evolution of a regular ...n of ridges in response to regional winds, and persistent wind ...gimes characteristic of the trade winds. With a lesser sand supply, isolated dunes such as *barchans* (crescentic, transverse features) or star-shaped dunes may occur, with barchans tending to occur in areas of more consistent wind direction than is the case for the pyramidal star-shaped dunes. Continuous systems of transverse dunes are associated with thick sand cover, or where sand flow is checked by a topographic barrier, by slackening wind velocities, or by vegetation. Other types of dune include those related to deposition behind or in front of topographic obstructions and those which are anchored by vegetation (Figure 11). Hairpin-shaped dunes, called *parabolics*, for example, arise when anchoring vegetation is present. Often, however, several different dune types may occur in close proximity and one dune type can grade into or develop from another. Thus Bagnold, in a classic study, demonstrated that the simple crescentic barchan can, by moving into an area with a different wind regime, become deformed into a linear *seif* dune. Likewise, a pair of linear dunes may develop when a parabolic dune is gradually elongated and a blow-out occurs at the 'nose' of the dune where the two parallel arms are connected. Thus

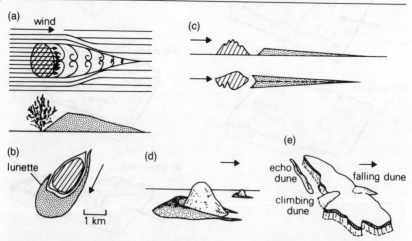

Figure 11 Obstacle or topographic dunes: (a) a small dune in the low velocity area to the lee of a shrub, (b) a crescentic lunette formed to the lee of a small desert depression, (c) dunes (wind-shadow dunes) in the lee of a hill, (d) dune to the windward of a hill, (e) dune development in the proximity of a plateau

the overemphasis of many textbooks on seifs and barchans is misleading and, indeed, barchans are in fact quite rare. It has been calculated that only 0.01 per cent of the sand in active dunes in the world's deserts is to be found in them. Another over-simplification is to divide dunes into either a transverse class or a longitudinal class: oblique forms are very common. Likewise, the importance of the grain size of the sand making up the dunes should not be missed. Dunes formed of coarse sand will be rounded and generally subdued and will have long wavelengths; where sands are well sorted and of intermediate grain size, the dunes tend to have a stronger relief and shorter wavelengths.

The sizes of sand dunes are also highly variable. Many linear dunes have a height of 5 to 30 m, but there are complex examples elsewhere that attain a height of 200 to 300 m. The spacing of such

Figure 12 A series of parallel linear dunes from the Wahiba Sand Sea (*erg*) in Oman

ridges (their wavelength) may vary from 200 to 5000 m, while individual ridges may extend for several hundreds of kilometres. Transverse ridges commonly have wavelengths of 50 to 200 m and heights up to 10 m, while some pyramidal dunes are up to 300 m high and between 1 and 2 km across.

The real importance of the different types of sand dune can be determined by analysing maps derived from Landsat satellite images (Table 2). Planimetric studies suggest on a world basis that the most important form of aeolian depositional surface is that of sand sheets and streaks with relatively ill-developed dune forms (about 38 per cent). Second in importance are miscellaneous types of linear dune (about 30 per cent), followed by crescentic dunes of predominantly barchanoid type (about 24 per cent), star dunes (5 per cent) and dome dunes (about 1 per cent). However, major regional differences arise between different sand seas (ergs). The Kalahari is notable for having a predominance of linear dunes (about 86 per cent), the Thar

	Thar	Takla Makan	Namib	Kalahari
A. Linear dunes (total)	14	22	33	86
simple and compound	14	19	18	86
feathered	–	–	–	–
with crescentic superimposed	–	3	–	–
with stars superimposed	–	–	14	–
B. Crescentic (total)	54	37	12	1
single barchanoid ridges	9	3	12	–
megabarchans	–	–	–	–
complex barchanoid ridges	17	34	–	–
parabolics	29	–	–	1
C. Star dunes	–	–	10	–
D. Dome dunes	–	7	–	–
E. Sheets and streaks	32	34	45	14
F. Undifferentiated	–	–	–	–

Note: The figures in this table give the percentages of the areas covered by different dune types.

Table 2 **Relative importance of major dune types in the world's deserts**

of India and Pakistan for having parabolics (about 29 per cent) and the north-east Sahara for having star dunes (about 24 per cent) (Figure 12).

The regularity in form of many linear dunes must be attributed to some regularity in the patterns of turbulence in the wind. Many workers believe that the long parallel ridges are formed by three-dimensional corkscrew-type threads of flow within the trade winds. These are called helical-roll vortices. These large-scale patterns are clearly seen on satellite images of sandy deserts but often have much larger wavelengths than the dunes they are supposed to mould. This model also implies that the formative winds are predominantly unidirectional, whereas analysis of wind data for many linear dune areas indicates that the winds are generally not unidirectional but bidirectional. A recent study of a linear dune in the Negev Desert by Tsoar, based on monitoring of sand and wind flow, has indicated that in the immediate lee of a linear dune crest the wind flow

Saudi Arabia	Ala Shan	South Sahara	North Sahara	North-east Sahara	West Sahara	Average
50	1	24	23	17	35	30.5
26	1	24	6	2	35	23.1
4	–	–	4	1	–	0.9
–	–	–	4	7	–	1.4
19	–	–	10	6	–	4.9
15	27	28	33	15	19	24.3
1	9	4	–	–	1	3.9
–	–	–	7	2	–	0.9
14	18	24	26	13	19	16.5
–	–	–	–	–	–	3.0
5	3	–	8	24	–	5.0
–	1	–	–	1	–	0.9
23	68	48	36	39	45	38.4
7	–	–	–	5	–	1.1

Table 2 continued

separates from the dune surface to create a lee side eddy, and that when crossing the crest at any angle whatsoever, the wind is deflected on the lee flank in the direction parallel to the crest line. Consequently Tsoar suggests that sand flow on the lee side of a linear dune is always along the dune. Secondly, Tsoar attempts to explain the broadly regular spacing of linear dunes by reference to the literature on wind breaks which suggests that the wind recovers its speed in the lee of an obstacle at a distance downwind of about 15 times the obstacle's height. Dune spacing may therefore be determined by dune height.

An important distinction between crescentic and linear dunes is that the former – generally barchans and parabolics – are often highly mobile compared with linear or star dunes which are virtually fixed landforms. In areas experiencing predominantly unidirectional winds, barchan dunes averaging about 5.0 m in height may move at rates approaching 30 m/year (Table 3).

At a continental scale, dunes show a remarkable regularity of pattern (see Figure 13). They tend to occur as a wheel-round or swirl in an anti-clockwise direction related to dominant continental wind patterns.

Location	Number of dunes (n)	Mean height (m)	Range in height (m)	Travel distance (m/year)
Peru	75	3.67	1.0−7.0	15.4
	42	4.38	1.2−6.0	14.2
	50	4.12	0.4−6.0	30.7
	114	3.0	−	30.0
Mexico	−	6.0	−	18.0
USA (California)	34	−	−	15.2
	47	5.89 (n = 27)	2.7−12.2 (n = 27)	25.0
Mauretania	44	8.8	3.0−17.0	30.0
Saudi Arabia	16	5.7	2.9−12.0	14.8
	67	8.54 (n = 56)	3.2−25.1 (n = 56)	14.64 (50 weeks)

Note: These data are based on the work of a number of scientists (Finkel, Hastenrath, Lettau & Lettau, Inman, Long, Sharp, Sarnthein, Walger, Fryberger and Watson)

Table 3 Barchan movement rates

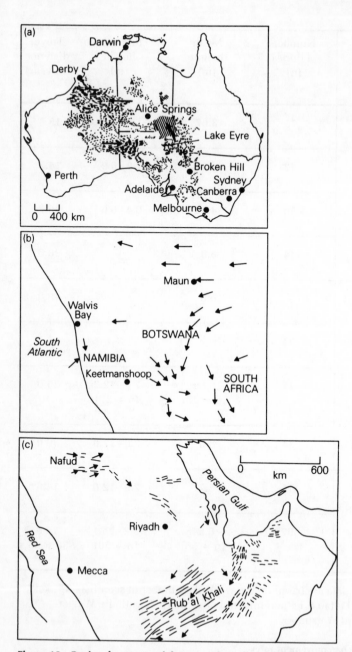

Figure 13 Regional patterns of dune trends to illustrate the characteristic wheel-round form. (a) Australia, (b) southern Africa, (c) Arabia

6. *Wind erosion in deserts*

The importance of wind in shaping deserts has been the subject of rapid changes of emphasis. At the end of the nineteenth century workers with experience in the windy, extremely dry Namib desert in southern Africa tended to see wind as the major process and attributed the formation of isolated mountains (*inselbergs*) to wind erosion. This has been termed the phase of 'extravagant aeolation'.

As a reaction against these views, and in part because of an increasing body of work from the high relief, tectonically active, and slightly wetter (semi-arid) deserts of North America, the role of wind was played down. Various arguments were used. Firstly, many of the wind-eroded features which were studied were found to be only minor or rare embellishments of forms produced by other processes. Features like ventifacts and zeugen are curiosities, not widespread desert forms. Secondly, some allegedly aeolian features, such as closed desert depressions, were shown to be caused by other processes, commonly tectonic. Thirdly, it was shown that many desert surfaces were protected from aeolian lowering by lag gravels or salt or clay crusts. Fourthly, the opinion was expressed that because wind erosion depends on the availability of abrasive sand (and saltating sand only moves at up to a metre or so above the ground surface) it only operates over a limited height range. Fifthly, analysis of wind records tended to discredit the notion of pervasive, strong winds. Finally, it was shown both that fluvial processes are currently very active in semi-desert areas because of the low infiltration capacity of surface materials, the limited vegetation cover, and the supposedly higher intensity rain storms, and that in pluvial periods their role was even greater and more widespread.

Many of these arguments are valid, but at the same time it is not correct to relegate the role of wind to an insignificant position, for there are various lines of evidence which point to its importance in certain deserts.

The examination of air photographs and satellite imagery has revealed that extensive areas of hard bedrock in the central Sahara, Iran, Peru, Arabia and north-west India possess huge arcuate grooves with relative relief of more than 100 m; these run for tens of kilometres, and have the same alignment as the prevailing winds. These are not minor features, even though they are yardangs (Figure 14).

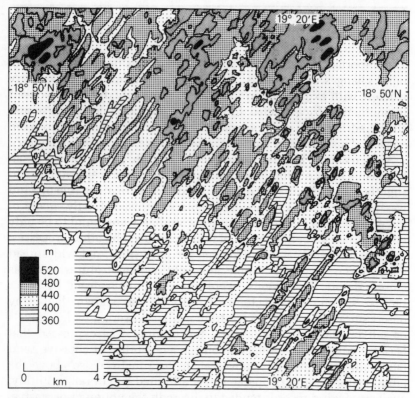

Figure 14 The pattern of wind eroded relief in the central Sahara. Note the considerable vertical relief, the persistence of the features, and their alignment in the direction of the north-east trades (after Hagedorn)

Likewise, the examination of desert depressions – *playas* – shows that they are large and frequent. There is no doubt that some, such as Death Valley in California, have a tectonic origin, while others may have a solutional origin (see p. 41), but many of them have a streamlined shape, occur in lines, have dunes on their lee sides resulting from the deposition of sediments excavated by wind from the hollows, and occur in certain topographic situations where wind erosion might be expected to be especially effective. The general association of so many hollows with deserts implies that 'normal' processes are inadequate to fill them in, and that some abnormal process (presumably wind) is effective at digging them out. As Peel (1966) has written: 'the volume of material excavated from the

Qattara I estimate roughly at some 800 cubic miles (3335 km³), and if this and similar depressions are truly the work of wind, it seems an overstatement to write it off as of little account as an agent of land-sculpture'.

Thirdly, an increasing number of meteorological observations at ground level or from satellites have demonstrated that dust storms (Figure 15), produced by the deflation of desert surfaces, are of frequent occurrence and cover large areas. In many desert areas, these are of sufficient density to reduce visibility to below 1000 m for 20 to 30 (exceptionally 60) days in the year (Figure 16), and dust plumes with dimensions of 2500 km × 600 km can be seen on satellite imagery. Rates of dust deposition in the east Atlantic between 10° and 25° S, brought about predominantly by deflation from the adjacent Sahara, average between 5 and 6 mm per 1000 years, while in March and April, 1960, one dust storm in the north Caucasus moved 960−1280 × 10⁶ tons of material, and the material settled in central Europe at distances of thousands of

Figure 15 One consequence of aeolian deflation is the dust storm. This example is taking place in Death Valley, California, and is removing silt and clay sized material from friable Pliocene deposits

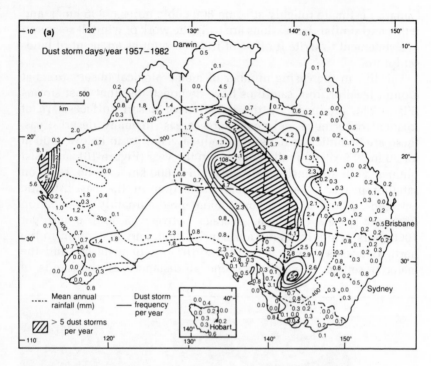

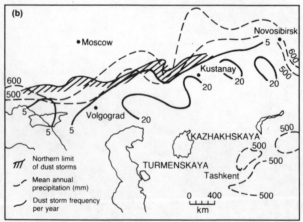

Figure 16 The frequency of dust storms per year which reduce visibility to less than 1000 m in (a) Australia (after Middleton), (b) southern USSR

kilometres. The great American dust storm of 12 November 1933, which heralded the Dust Bowl years, covered an area from the Canadian boundary, southward to the western Ohio and lower Missouri valleys, a region of greater extent than the combined areas of France, Italy and Hungary. Later on in the 1930s, because of a combination of severe drought and inappropriate agricultural practices, the dust storms occurred with unprecedented frequency. The area is in no sense desert, but by leaving large areas bare of vegetation the farmers had matched the vegetation-free surface of a desert.

In April 1935 Amarillo in Texas had 28 days in the month with dust storms. Likewise, during the Sahel drought of the early 1970s, the quantity of dust moved from the southern margins of the Sahara and transported to the Atlantic (even as far as Barbados) was three times higher than it was before the drought.

Finally, it is worth mentioning that during the cold phases (glacials) of the last Ice Age, while some areas were wetter, large areas of the tropics and subtropics were even drier than they are now and more sand movement took place. This would have increased the amount of wind abrasion that occurred. Moreover, studies of an ice core in Greenland show that during the last glaciation (prior to 10 000 years ago) the amount of aeolian dust that was being deposited was about 100 times higher than in the Holocene (the last 10 000 years).

7. Climatic change in deserts

The events which led to the frequent and substantial expansions (glacials) and contractions (interglacials) of the great ice sheets and mountain glaciers in the Ice Age (Pleistocene period), also led to major environmental changes in lower latitudes. The shifting of the windbelts caused changes in precipitation, the whole nature of the atmospheric general circulation was modified, and temperatures and associated evaporation rates were altered.

During the glacial maxima, desert conditions appear to have been more extensive than now, and active sand dune fields (ergs) may have characterised as much as 50 per cent of the land area between 30° N and 30° S, compared to a present level of about 10 per cent. Dunes extended into areas that are now savanna or rainforest, and under the present conditions of relative humidity these dunes have become degraded and weathered but are still readily identified on aerial photographs and satellite imagery. The degree of change in precipitation that these ancient ergs suggest can be gauged from the fact that active dunes can only form where vegetation cover is greatly reduced (that is, in areas where rainfall is less than about 250 mm/year). The ancient dunes occur where the precipitation today may be well in excess of 750 mm/year.

Confirmatory evidence of periods of former greater aridity is provided by ocean cores, which show in their sedimentary record accelerated deflational activity and dust storm development on neighbouring land areas. In addition, studies of lake cores in certain tropical areas have shown that there have been phases of greater salinity and of more xerophytic vegetation at some times in the Pleistocene.

However, many desert areas have undergone changes other than towards greater aridity, for inter-pluvials have alternated with periods of greater humidity called pluvials or lacustrals. Indeed, the presence of greater precipitation in the past has been inferred from miscellaneous pieces of evidence: the presence of remains of human habitation in areas now too dry for man to survive; the distribution of animal and plant remains in isolated patches which must formerly have been united; the extension of vast river systems which are currently inactive and choked by dune fields; the presence of fossil soils and weathering horizons of humid type; the presence of spreads of spring tufas, indicating higher ground-water levels; and, above all, the geomorphological evidence of high lake levels in closed basins.

The evidence of such expanded lakes is widespread. Notable examples are to be found in the currently saline basins of the Basin-and-Range Province of the south-west United States. Lake Bonneville, for instance, now 2600–6500 km² in area, reached 52 000 km² and was 335 m deeper than it is now. Similarly, the Aral and Caspian Seas united to form a lake covering 1 100 000 km², the Dead Sea in the Middle East was 220 m deeper than it is now, and Lake Chad, on the Sahara margins, expanded some hundreds of kilometres from its present desiccated state.

The difficult question is, when did these great environmental changes take place? It used to be thought that the cold events of high latitudes were contemporaneous with the pluvials in deserts, and in some areas this is true, but there is an increasing body of evidence from low latitude deserts that the dry phases tended to occur at times of maximum glaciation. Radiocarbon dates suggest that a major phase of relative aridity occurred over large parts of Africa, Australia, tropical South America, and northern India, between about 25 000 and 12 000 years ago; the maximum of the last glaciation in the northern hemisphere was at about 18 000 to 17 000 years ago, and glaciers retreated rapidly after about 11 000 years ago. Pluvials from the same areas, which appear to have been frequent but relatively short-lived, have also been dated by radio-carbon with the last major pluvial occurring in the early Holocene (post-glacial) around 9000 years ago. However, in south-west USA the high lake levels coincide more closely with the last glaciation, reflecting the more southerly tracks of depressions and reduced evaporation with lower temperatures.

That great changes of climate have taken place is seldom disputed. The relationship between the development of landforms and these climatic changes is often more problematical, except in the relatively clear-cut cases of ancient dunes and high lake shorelines. This is brought out strongly in a consideration of alternations between periods of *fluvial incision* (*gullying*) and *aggradation* (terrace and fan formation). Aggradation, for example, could result from a reduced vegetation cover (brought about by aridity) which permitted a greater sediment load to be delivered to stream channels, from increased rates of frost weathering (which could have the same effect), from tectonic activity, from base level changes, from increased rainfall (which could also deliver coarser sediments to stream channels) or from decreased rainfall (which could lead to aeolian sediments choking fluvial systems). Incision, on the other hand, could result from catastrophic storms, from the removal of a protective vegetation layer, from tectonic uplift, and so on. Moreover, incision in the upper part of a catchment might, by providing increased sediment yield, lead to deposition (and terrace formation) downstream.

It is likely, especially in old shield areas and on ancient erosion surfaces, that the imprint of climatic changes goes back beyond the Pleistocene. Thus, in Australia, the presence of ancient weathering crusts (duricrusts), including laterite, in desert areas, is probably to be attributed to more humid conditions which existed in the Cretaceous to the early Cainozoic, and the same applies to some major drainage lines which are infilled with Eocene sediments.

This problem of the significance of climatic change in moulding landforms and controlling the operation of geomorphic processes has been heightened in recent years because of widespread concern as to whether deserts are expanding. This theme of desertisation or desertification on desert margins has led to a controversy as to whether the alleged spread of desert-like conditions involving dune encroachment, increased soil erosion, and a greater frequency of dust storms, is the result of climatic deterioration, or human mismanagement caused by overgrazing, deforestation and burning of vegetation. In all probability, the phenomenon results largely from the fact that increasing population pressures lead to an increasing level of vegetation removal which in turn makes the land surface more prone to erosive processes during years of adverse climatic conditions. Thus the Sahel drought of the late 1960s and early 1970s was not notably more extreme than previously recorded droughts in the twentieth century, but, because of the greatly increased population of both humans and their domestic animals, the effects were considerably worse. On the other hand, the changes in albedo related to vegetation loss could trigger more fundamental changes in the future.

8. *Explaining desert landforms: equifinality and uniqueness*

Equifinality

One of the main lessons that can be gained from the study of desert landforms is that features which have a broadly similar form may have been created by processes which are fundamentally rather diverse. Simple or single explanations are often not appropriate. This can be illustrated by a consideration of certain common desert landforms.

Stone pavements

These consist of so-called armoured surfaces composed of relatively coarse rock fragments which lie above sediment containing much more fine material, such as sand, silt and clay.

The standard explanation is that the coarse surface material is the product of deflation of fine materials by wind. Such removal of the bulk of the fine material from a deposit which originally contained a large range of grain sizes would tend to leave the coarse contents as a lag or residue.

However, an equally plausible explanation is that the coarse materials could remain at the surface after fine sediments had been initially dislodged by rain splash and had then been flushed away by running water in the form of sheet floods.

Both these mechanisms require the *lateral* removal of fines, but coarse materials might equally well arrive at the surface as a concentration if some vertical sorting process took place. Such vertical movement could be brought about by frost action, by wetting and drying, or by the alternate hydration and dehydration of salts in saline soils.

Closed depressions

The range of possible hypotheses to explain the origin of closed depressions is even larger, but once again a popular (and important) mechanism is that of deflation. This involves the removal of susceptible sediments, perhaps produced by weathering processes such as salt crystallisation, from areas of bare ground by wind. Such depressions may show characteristic alignments, wind-moulded shapes, and crescentic dunes produced by deposition of material excavated from the depression on their lee sides. Many hollows, both large (e.g. the Qattara depression with a volume of 3335 km^3 and a depth reaching 134 m below sea level) and small may be formed by this process.

However, many closed depressions, such as some of those in the south-west United States, are essentially the result of block faulting, while the large basins in shield and platform areas, for example that of Lake Chad, are caused by a broader-scale tectonic warping. Fluvial processes have not been sufficiently powerful to fill them in completely.

Alternatively, some hollows, particularly the *dayas* of limestone surfaces in Morocco and elsewhere, may result from solution processes (possibly dating back to pluvial phases), while in southern Africa and other semi-desert areas it has been suggested that animal activity may have contributed. The animals would tend to concentrate around any small hollow where water might accumulate, and by pawing and removal of mud on their bodies would tend to enlarge the initial depression; such features are known as buffalo wallows in the USA.

Yet other basins may have an essentially depositional origin. Basins impounded by barriers of wind-blown sand, for example, are characteristic of flat plains and valley floors near the margins of dune fields or towards the end of a drainage system, where aeolian sand has invaded and blocked river systems.

Gully development

In many desert areas, recent years have seen the development of deep gully systems incised into older valley fills of alluvium.

A commonly advocated cause of gully formation is that of increased discharge brought about by climatic change.

An alternative possibility is that vegetation removal and alteration could have been achieved by the action of man: grazing of sheep and cattle, fire, and deforestation. Such vegetation removal would lead to exposure of ground to erosion and might also promote greater surface runoff.

A further mechanism involves the focusing of runoff by man-made structures such as roads and railways. Roads, for example, being largely impermeable in comparison with natural surfaces, could generate runoff which, if carelessly conducted onto susceptible alluvium, might cause a gully to form.

Some gullying may be promoted by tectonic disturbance. An area of newly-uplifted ground might be subject to incision.

Alternatively, some gullies might be created by a catastrophic flood event of high magnitude and low frequency.

Pediments

These are gently sloping surfaces (generally between 1° and 7°), usually slightly concave in longitudinal profile, cut in bedrock, and with only a thin veneer of detritus. There is often a sharp break of slope between the mountain front and the pediment at its base. Once again many hypotheses have been advanced to explain them.

One of the first hypotheses was that they were cut by wind erosion. This, it was felt, could both undercut steep slopes and remove the finer products of rock disintegration. Such a mechanism could conceivably account for some of the pediments of almost nil gradient which occur in the Tibesti area of the Sahara.

Another early hypothesis was that they were formed by sheet-floods which pared down the surface to give a relatively undissected, gently sloping surface. Such sheetfloods do occur, but it needs to be remembered that whatever the effects of such rare sheetfloods may be, they cannot create the pediment surface, for a relatively smooth, undissected gentle slope is a prerequisite for their establishment. This particular hypothesis would thus seem to involve an element of circular reasoning.

Yet another water-related hypothesis has explained pediments as being the result of lateral planation. Under this mechanism it is envisaged that streams emerging from the mountain front would be free to swing from side to side and to erode the surface, but it does not really explain pediments that directly abut the mountain front (as many do) away from such swinging channels.

A fourth pediment hypothesis relies on the assumption that sub-surface weathering is likely to be accentuated at the junction between the mountain front and the plain because of the natural concentration of water there through percolation. This, it is held, will lead to preferential weathering at the break of slope, undercutting of the mountain front, and the provision of weathered debris that can then be removed by sheetflow, wind and other processes.

We could give many further examples of the variety of hypotheses that can be put forward to explain desert landforms, and we have also touched upon this theme in connection with desert crusts (see p. 19). Suffice it to say that we often do not have adequate knowledge to come down firmly on the side of any one hypothesis, that landforms are complex and may be formed by combinations of different processes, and that an hypothesis that applies in one desert may not apply in another.

Are desert landforms unique?

As we have made clear in the first chapter, desert landforms are highly variable in type, distribution and assemblage. One cannot talk of any one desert landscape, We have also made it clear that deserts have a long history and that some of their features have developed under different climates from those of today. We have also indicated that desert landscapes are far from being the products of processes that are specific to deserts. Wind erosion, deflation and insolation weathering are by no means the only contemporary processes; water action may be as important as (and in some cases probably more important than) it is in more humid areas. Thus, if desert landscapes are different from those of 'normal' areas, the difference is likely to be essentially one of degree, while some of the difference may be more apparent than real; the relative absence of vegetation can make the landscape look more angular than it does in a humid area when in reality it may not be so. Some of the terminology of desert geomorphology, peppered as it is with words from languages as diverse as Arabic, Tibetan and German, tends to give some credence to notions of the uniqueness of desert landforms, but it is as well to remember that, for example, a *wadi* is a river.

Many of the landforms of deserts can be found in other environments, either because the same processes operate in other environments or because different processes may play a similar role. Thus in periglacial areas ice may lead to the physical disintegration of rock in a way that may be very broadly analogous to salt weathering in a desert. Likewise, patterned ground produced by desiccation cracking of surface sediments in deserts has a strong resemblance to periglacial patterned ground produced by fluctuations in the volume of ice-rich soil in cold areas of the world. Indeed, many of the features of desert landscapes that are often thought of as characteristic or even diagnostic are found elsewhere: alluvial fans are common in tundra areas and on the flanks of glacial troughs; inselbergs are found in some of the wettest areas of the world as well as the driest; stone pavements are a feature of some periglacial sediments, and storms raise dust from glacial outwash plains. Indeed, wind-blown loess from such areas reaches great thickness.

One can, however, probably regard the action of wind as a true desert process, resulting in the formation of unmistakable arid landforms. Wind erosion occurs under freak conditions in temperate zones when, for example, ploughed farmland is subjected to drought and windy conditions, but it is only in deserts with dominantly uni-directional winds that large-scale erosional landscapes develop. These features have few counterparts in non-desert terrain, except perhaps the ephemeral snow ridges (zastrugi) of arctic regions. Similarly, extensive dune fields are not found in areas other than deserts unless they are fossil features which developed under desert conditions in the past, or coastal features, which in any case have a much more restricted occurrence.

9. The human impact

Human activities are an increasingly important cause of change in desert landscapes and on desert margins. There are various reasons for this: human technological changes, such as the introduction of ever larger and more sophisticated irrigation methods, are placing new stresses on the environment; life styles are changing, with, for example, sparse nomadic populations tending to become settled and desert cities to grow; deserts are being exposed to an increasing array of uses, including oil exploitation, military testing, recreation, and so on; new areas are being populated and developed and for many of them the amount of reliable environmental information is small.

The nature of the human impact on deserts can be illustrated by some selected examples.

Ground subsidence

The removal of fluids from beneath the ground surface can lead to gradual ground subsidence. There are two prime causes of this phenomenon in desert areas: ground-water abstraction and hydro-carbon (oil and gas) exploitation. Ground-water abstraction occurs to provide water for irrigation and for municipal and industrial supplies. If the amount of water that is pumped out of the ground exceeds the rate at which it is recharged by the sparse desert rainfall, the level of the water table will fall, and this in turn will promote ground subsidence. Classic areas for this problem are the rich agricultural land of the Central Valley of California in the USA (where over 8.9 m of subsidence has occurred) and the basin in which Mexico City lies (over 7.5 m of subsidence). It is important to realise that this is approximately equal to the height of a normal two storey house. The subsidence causes structural collapse of buildings and utilities, makes areas prone to flooding (especially if they are close to sea-level), and destroys the carefully arranged levels of gravity-fed irrigation schemes. Even more significant is the fact that once subsidence has occurred, the underlying aquifer becomes compacted and loses its potential for ground-water recharge. A classic area for subsidence produced by oil and gas abstraction is Long Beach near Los Angeles, in California, where over 9 m of subsidence took place in just over 40 years.

Downstream effects of dams

To reduce the consequences of droughts, to lessen the effects of floods, and to provide power, many desert rivers are being straddled by dams. These dams are becoming increasingly large, and increasingly numerous. It is probable that around 700 dams are being built world-wide each year at the present time. Moreover, by 1990 the world-wide total of dams greater than 150 m in height reached 113, of which 49 were built in the 1980s.

Such dams have numerous geomorphic consequences. A particularly important consequence of impounding a reservoir behind a dam is the reduction in the sediment load of the river downstream. The Aswan High Dam and Lake Nasser have caused the Nile's load downstream to be reduced to just 8 per cent of natural levels. Sediment removal at this scale in turn has various possible consequences: accelerated river bed erosion since there is less sediment available to cause bed aggradation, and accelerated coastal erosion because beaches and deltas are no longer replenished by fluvial sediment inputs. The Nile Delta has retreated by around 1.6 km in half a century as a consequence of control of its flow by a succession of dams and barrages.

There is also evidence that large reservoirs can increase seismic activity. With the ever increasing number and size of reservoirs the threat increases. The reasons why reservoirs induce earthquakes include the depression of the earth's crust caused by the mass of water in the reservoir, and the changing water pressures across the contact surfaces of faults.

Flood control works and major diversions of river water for irrigation will also cause inevitable changes in the nature of river channels downstream. This can be shown for the North Platte and the South Platte rivers in Nebraska, USA, where both peak discharge and mean annual discharge have declined to 10 to 30 per cent of their pre-dam values. The North Platte, 762 to 1219 m wide in 1890 has narrowed to about 60 m at present, while the South Platte, which was 792 m wide 89 km upstream from its junction with the North Platte in 1897 had narrowed to about 60 m in 1959. The tendency for both rivers has been to form one narrow, well defined, sinuous channel in place of the previously wide, braided channels.

Accelerated salt weathering

As explained earlier (see p. 15), rocks (and building materials) often disintegrate very rapidly in the presence of salt in desert environments. Thus, if human activities cause an increase in salinity, the rate of rock weathering and building decay may accelerate. An example of this is provided by the 4000 year old archaeological site of Mohenjo-Daro in Pakistan. This ancient city, built of burnt brick, has suffered catastrophic decay in recent decades as a consequence of the spread of irrigation in the Indus Plain. The construction of barrages and the excavation of irrigation canals have enabled the area of cultivation to be expanded. However, the application of large amounts of water to the ground surface and the seepage of water from the canals, has caused the ground-water level in the alluvium of the plain to rise sharply. As its level approaches the ground surface the ascending water is subjected to extreme evaporation under the hot, dry atmospheric conditions, with those minerals dissolved in the water becoming increasingly concentrated. Eventually the concentration becomes such that salts are precipitated at the ground surface, attacking building materials with which they come into contact. It has become necessary to try and reduce the level of the water table artificially by means of a ring of boreholes and pumps around the archaeological site.

Desertification

It is evident from the work of archaeologists and historians that in the past many marginal, semi-arid regions had the potential to support significant human populations. Agricultural production in the northern Sahara was of major importance to the Roman Empire and pre-Roman societies in the region. Yet, though these areas had a great potential for agricultural production, today little cultivation is attempted. Whether the climate of the region at that time was more conducive to agriculture, or whether the technology employed then was more suited to the fragile environment, is unknown. Throughout North Africa and the Middle East, there are numerous examples of former cities, towns and villages now abandoned – even some buried beneath desert sand dunes. In Arabia alone, tens of thousands of hectares of formerly productive agricultural land are barren today. The same is true in Iran, Afghanistan, Pakistan and the arid parts of India.

This process of degradation of agricultural economies in the world's semi-arid regions is today of major concern. It is apparent that through either natural forces, such as climatic fluctuations, or through human influences, such as rapid population growth or mismanagement of natural resources, many formerly fertile environments are becoming increasingly less productive. The symptoms are far more obvious than the causes: desertification of the Sahel; devastation of livestock populations; mass starvation in Ethiopia and Sudan. While the most immediate cause may be perceived as drought, or a series of drier than average years, such climatic events probably are not aberrant when viewed over the long-term. The natural forces involved in present worldwide desertification are probably no different from those which have occurred many times in the past. Today, however, human forces have a far stronger influence than ever before. Formerly, populations responded to droughts and famine by adopting more nomadic agricultural practices. Such a response is not feasible in many areas today because of increased population density and the presence of national boundaries. Population pressure in itself probably exacerbates the process of desertification and its consequences. Population increase promotes overstocking of livestock and the expansion of cultivated land into less productive, more marginal areas. Crops in these areas will be the first to fail in times of drought, leaving areas devoid of trees and other natural vegetation adapted to withstand the stress. The bare land surface may then be subjected to erosion which removes the potentially fertile topsoil.

It is impossible to identify all of the factors which contribute to the process of desertification. However, the misapplication of modern technology has had a significant influence in numerous areas. Many attempts to bring marginal land into agricultural production have been ill-conceived because they have not taken periodic extremes in climate into consideration. For example, the widespread installation of drilled water-wells in rural areas of Africa enabled farmers greatly to increase their livestock numbers as drinking water for the animals became available. Yet though the sufficiency of drinking water is a major factor limiting livestock density in years with average rainfall, the availability of grazing is most critical during drier than average years. Most of the deep wells are not productive enough to supply irrigation water as well as drinking water. Hence, during drought years there is insufficient grazing to support the livestock population.

Notwithstanding the possible deleterious effects that the introduction of modern technology can have on economies or environments to which it is not suited, innovative agricultural practices can play a beneficial role in the Third World. Provided that water resources are used prudently the drilling of deep wells often proves an invaluable asset to rural communities in semi-arid areas. Moreover, the development of hybrid varieties of food plants and livestock better adapted to arid conditions, can extend the area of land which can be brought into sustained agricultural production. However, the dire consequences of overstepping the environmental limitations in these marginal areas cannot be overstated.

Beyond the Third World, cultural and economic constraints on development are often less pronounced and the agricultural potential of semi-arid lands is still greater. Large-scale, mechanised farming techniques, the use of chemicals to reduce salinity problems and fertilisers to raise crop yields, have greatly increased the area of productive farmland in many regions. Again, however, over exploitation can have dramatic consequences. The short-term benefits in crop yields gained by irrigating can be completely negated if excessive soil salinisation results, since this can make the land unproductive for decades. Similarly, the erosion of fertile topsoil by wind and water is a problem which is often exacerbated by large-scale, mechanised farming practices.

In the past, the consequences of severe drought – the depletion of both livestock and human populations – were accepted as a natural response to the desert environment. Today, in regions where population pressure is great, immediate solutions to the problems of drought are not available since the relocation of human populations is impractical. In the long-term, the successful exploitation of marginal lands in the semi-arid regions of the Third World will necessitate improved education of rural populations, especially with regard to land management and agricultural practices. However, before such major changes can be implemented the problems posed by continuing population growth must be alleviated. Solutions to these seemingly intractable problems require fundamental changes in the socio-economic structure of the cultures – changes which are necessarily slow.

As we have seen, the application of modern technology to the farming practices in semi-arid regions can provide major benefits. However, even in the most technologically advanced farming economies, mismanagement of natural resources is not uncommon.

Indeed, the introduction of innovative farming techniques accelerated the development of the North American Dust Bowl in the 1930s. Even today, over exploitation of deep ground-water resources such as the Ogallala-aquifer of the American Midwest bodes a troubled future for agriculture in the hub of the wheat-belt. In some areas the Ogallala is being depleted at twice the rate of its recharge. Elsewhere in the south-western United States, ground-water levels are falling at alarming rates – up to 6.0 m/year in the San Joachin Valley of California – and irrigation water is being pumped from depths of more than 1000 m. Around Tucson, Arizona, ground-water is being exploited at five times the rate of its natural recharge. Today in Saudi Arabia the attainment of self-sufficiency in wheat production is being heralded as a major achievement. Here also production is at great cost to ground-water resources and future water supplies are jeopardised because of current over-exploitation. While some have argued that large-scale mining of ground-water exemplifies man's ability to overcome natural restraints on the development of arid regions, others have pointed out that such technological remedies are often illusory since they promote greater problems in the long term.

Innovative technology is not a panacea for the agricultural problems of the semi-arid and arid regions of the globe. Without careful consideration of the environmental impact of new technologies, the detrimental effects of climatic fluctuations may be compounded. Moreover, as human capability to exploit the natural environment increases, the ability of such environments to recover from mismanagement and over-exploitation diminishes.

10. The application of desert geomorphology

A striking feature of research in desert geomorphology is that there has been a long standing concern with the application of this research to matters that have social, economic or engineering significance. There are two prime reasons for this: the need to avoid natural and quasi-natural hazards, and the need to find and develop natural resources.

Arid areas are characterised by a very wide range of geomorphological and hydrological hazards. A selection of these is listed in Table 4. Some of these hazards are termed quasi-natural, being caused or exacerbated by human activities of the type described in the last section. If arid areas are to be developed successfully the distribution, nature, severity and causes of these hazards need to be appreciated, not least because some of them are unfamiliar to engineers and agriculturalists who have been trained in other environments.

Let us take two examples from aeolian geomorphology to see what can be done: encroaching sand dunes and wind erosion of soils. Moving sand dunes may encroach upon agricultural land, they may migrate into and fill irrigation canals, they may block lines of communication, and they may overwhelm engineering structures such as oil pipe-lines. It is therefore necessary to be able to identify

Flooding of valleys, fans and playas	Sedimentation behind dams	Calcretization
Sabkha inundation	Clear water erosion downstream from dams	Desiccation contraction
Hydrocompaction	Salt weathering	Dune encroachment and reactivation
	Gully development	
	Piping	
Surface subsidence due to water and hydrocarbon extraction	Landslides, rock falls and related slope failure phoneomena	Visibility reduction by dust
		Soil erosion

Table 4 **Examples of geomorphological hazards in deserts**

those areas where dunes are migrating and to try and assess in which direction they are moving and how fast. This may be done by field monitoring with such devices as stakes, and by mapping their positions by the use of sequential air photography. Once the threat has been identified it may be necessary to establish the most suitable means by which the dunes may be stopped, deflected, or rendered less dangerous. In recent years, as Table 5 indicates, a whole array of techniques has been developed to this end.

---

1 *Drifting sand*
  Enhancement of deposition of sand by the creation of large ditches, vegetation belts and barriers and fences.
  Enhancement of transport of sand by aerodynamic streamlining of the surface, change of surface materials or panelling to direct flow.
  Reduction of sand supply, by surface treatment, improved vegetation cover or erection of fences.
  Deflection of moving sand, by fences, barriers, tree belts, etc.
2 *Moving dunes*
  Removal by mechanical excavation.
  Destruction by reshaping, trenching through dune axis or surface stabilisation of barchan arms.
  Immobilisation, by trimming, surface treatment and fences.

Table 5 **Methods available to attempt to control drifting sand and moving dunes**

Soil erosion by wind is a severe problem in areas like the High Plains of America or the Mallee of Australia, partly because of the loss of top soil that occurs, and partly because the dust storms generated by the deflation of such top soils can have undesirable consequences such as the disruption of road and air traffic. The applied geomorphologist may contribute to the solution of such problems by determining and mapping those particular soil and surface material types which are especially prone to deflation. These may include areas of friable silty alluvium, or areas of ancient wind-blown silt, called loess. Once such areas have been established the recommendation can be made that the development of them should be carried out with extreme caution. Secondly, an understanding of the fundamental processes involved in deflation may permit an assessment of the most appropriate form of land-use and the most appropriate types of remedial action. For example, in planting shelterbelts as windbreaks it is important that the alignment is correctly related to the local wind conditions that cause erosion, that the spacing of the belts is optimal, and that the heights and density of the belts is correct. Likewise, experiments may demonstrate which cultivation techniques (for example, the type and time of ploughing, the amount of stubble that should be left, and so on) give the most resistant soil structure to reduce the threat of soil erosion.

The other role of the applied geomorphologist is to find resources for the construction industry, and to help with the mapping of soil types. The mapping of landforms is crucial in this endeavour, for surface material types are closely related to landform. For example, particular types of aggregate may be found in association with particular geomorphological features. Alluvial fans may provide a source of gravel, calcrete outcrops may provide a source of lime or of road-making material, playa lakes may provide a source of particular types of salt, while dunes, alluvial deposits, and old shorelines may provide sands of varying character. Likewise, the

Figure 17 A salt-damaged building in Bahrain. Capillary rise has brought saline ground-water up into the foundations, and salt crystal growth has caused the concrete to decay

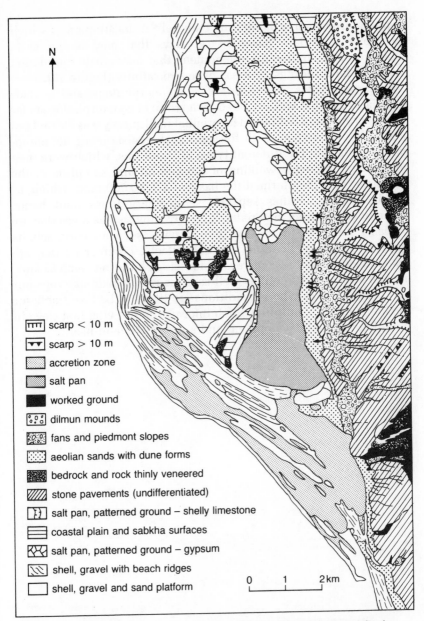

Legend:

- scarp < 10 m
- scarp > 10 m
- accretion zone
- salt pan
- worked ground
- dilmun mounds
- fans and piedmont slopes
- aeolian sands with dune forms
- bedrock and rock thinly veneered
- stone pavements (undifferentiated)
- salt pan, patterned ground – shelly limestone
- coastal plain and sabkha surfaces
- salt pan, patterned ground – gypsum
- shell, gravel with beach ridges
- shell, gravel and sand platform

0   1   2 km

Figure 18 A portion of a map of the geomorphology and surface materials of Bahrain prepared at a scale of 1:50,000 by the geomorphologists of the Bahrain Surface Materials Resource Survey

mapping of particular landforms may help in locating areas which are prone to certain hazards, e.g. clays that may be prone to expansion and contraction phenomena that may create foundation problems for buildings, or areas of severe salinity (Figure 17).

Figure 18 shows a portion of a geomorphology and surface materials map that was prepared by a group of geomorphologists for the Government of Bahrain. The original field survey was carried out at a scale of 1:10 000, with the geomorphologists using air photographs to delimit the different types of landforms, which were then checked by intensive walking of the ground and sampling of the materials. This then formed the basis of a 1:50 000 map, which, as can be seen, identifies separate sedimentary types (and hence different engineering materials). It clearly shows some areas that are palpably unsuited to construction activity (such as salty, sabkha surfaces, prone to flooding and salt attack), other areas that are potential sources of fine aggregates for use in building (such as fans, aeolian sands, and so on) as well as areas where bedrock crops out and provides sites where conditions are likely to be favourable for the foundations of building. Such information is a vital first stage in planning regional development and appropriate land-use.

Topics for discussion

1 Which geomorphological processes that operate in deserts do you think might be hazardous to man?

2 In what ways has man altered the landforms and geomorphological processes of desert regions?

3 Obtain a good atlas with relief maps at a scale of between 1 : 500 000 and 1 : 5 000 000 of some desert areas (for example, Australia, south-west USA, the Sahara). What are the main relief features you can identify at this scale? To what extent do the deserts appear to vary?

4 Place some roughly equally-sized lumps of rock (preferably chalk, limestone or sandstone, weighing around 50 to 100 g) into glass beakers (one lump per beaker) after you have weighed them. Pour over them a saturated solution of a salt, preferably magnesium sulphate (Epsom salts) or sodium sulphate (Glauber's salt). Let the solution soak in for an hour, then pour off the solution and let the samples dry off in a cool oven. Repeat this for ten or twenty days and then re-weigh the lumps. Record the loss of weight for different rock types. What process is responsible?

5 Where in Britain might you find some of the landforms found in deserts?

6 How might you tell whether or not climate had changed in a desert area?

7 Attempt to design experiments whereby you could ascertain the direction and speed of movement of sand dunes.

8 If you had to build a road in a desert area what types of relief would you avoid?

9 How does the nature of the vegetation cover affect geomorphological processes in deserts?

10 Consider the climatic statistics for desert stations on page 58. By reference to such controls as latitude, altitude and continentality try to account for their differences. Also, to what extent do you think that different geomorphological processes may operate in these different desert types?

Station	J	F	M	A	M	J	J	A	S	O	N	D	YEAR
Chimbay	−6.2	−4.1	2	12	19.6	24.2	26.2	24	17.5	9.7	0.9	−4.7	10.1
(USSR) 66 m	7	14	13	12	10	6	2	2	3	7	5	8	89
Bahrain	17.4	18.3	21.2	25.6	29.6	32	33.8	34.3	32.5	29	24.5	19.2	26.4
2 m	16	15	11	6	1	0	0	0	0	0	9	18	76
Aden	25.5	25.6	27.2	28.7	30.7	32.8	32.2	31.6	31.7	28.9	26.6	26	28.9
(S. Yemen) 3 m	7	3	6	0	1	0	3	2	7	1	3	6	39
Jodhpur	17.1	19.9	25.2	30.3	34.4	34.3	31.3	29.2	29.4	27.7	22.7	18.7	26.7
(India) 224 m	8	5	2	2	6	31	122	146	47	7	3	1	38
Alice Springs	28.2	27.4	24.7	20.2	15.5	12.4	11.9	14.1	18.2	22.6	25.4	27.6	20.7
(Australia) 548 m	27	45	18	10	18	15	14	10	6	25	23	39	25
Lima	21.5	22.3	20.1	17.8	16.0	15.3	15.1	15.4	16.3	17.7	19.4	21.5	18.2
(Peru) 155 m	1	0.4	0.6	0.4	6	4	6	7	6	2	1	0.8	35
Kashgar	−5.3	−0.6	7.6	15.4	21	24.9	26.7	25.8	21.3	14	5.3	−2.5	12.9
(China) 1310 m	15	13	13	5	8	5	10	8	3	3	5	8	86

Notes:
The altitude of each station is given in metres. The top row of statistics are mean monthly temperatures (in degrees centigrade), while the lower row of figures are mean monthly precipitation levels (in millimetres).

Bibliography and further reading

A brief guide to the general geography of deserts is provided by A. S. Goudie and J. C. Wilkinson, 1977, *The Warm Desert Environment*, Cambridge University Press.

A much more extensive guide, strong on Soviet examples, is M. P. Petrov, 1976, *Deserts of the World*, Halsted Press.

Three textbooks which expand upon the theme of desert geomorphology are R. U. Cooke and A. Warren, 1973, *Geomorphology in Deserts*, Batsford; J. A. Mabbutt, 1977, *Desert Landforms*, M.I.T. Press and D. S. G. Thomas (ed.), 1989, *Arid-zone Geomorphology*, Belhaven Press.

The role of the human impact is discussed in A. S. Goudie, 1990, *The Human Impact on the Environment*, Basil Blackwell, while the importance of natural hazards and applied geomorphology is expertly treated in R. U. Cooke, D. Brunsden, J. C. Doornkamp, and D. K. C. Jones, 1982, *Urban Geomorphology in Drylands*, Oxford University Press.

A good general assessment of the resources and problems of land use in arid lands is provided by R. L. Heathcote, 1983, *The Arid Lands: Their Use and Abuse*, Longman.

The following works are referred to in the text:
Uwe George, 1978, *In the Deserts of this Earth*, Hamish Hamilton.

J. A. Mabutt, 1977, *Desert Landforms*, M.I.T. Press.

R. F. Peel, 1966, 'The Landscape in aridity', *Transactions*, The Institute of British Geographers.

A. S. Goudie, in A. F. Pitty (ed.), 1985, *Themes in Geomorphology*, p. 128, Croom Helm.